BROTHE

A guide for young children
Written by Hedi Argent

Illustrations by Maggie Chamberlain (age 7)
and Emil Chamberlain (age 5), p15

Acknowledgements

I am grateful to Shelley Dorffman and her colleagues at Coram's Adoption Service for commenting on the text and testing it out with a family; to Shaila Shah, BAAF Director of Publications for publishing it and making it look good and to Abi Omotoso for editing it. But most of all, I want to thank all the children who have adopted and taught me what it means, especially Poppy who read an early draft and gave me helpful tips. This book is dedicated to her and her "baby bother".

Published by
British Association for Adoption & Fostering (BAAF)
Saffron House
6-10 Kirby Street
London EC1N 8TS
www.baaf.org.uk

Charity registration 275689 (England and Wales) and SC039337 (Scotland)
© Hedi Argent, 2010
Reprinted 2010

British Library Cataloguing in Publication Data
A catalogue record for this book is available from the British Library

ISBN 978 1 907585 00 5

Project management by Abi Omotoso, BAAF
All photographs posed by models

Designed and typeset by Helen Joubert Design
Illustrations by Maggie and Emil Chamberlain
Printed in Great Britain by The Lavenham Press
Trade distribution by Turnaround Publisher Services, Unit 3, Olympia Trading Estate, Coburg Road, London N22 6TZ

BAAF is the leading UK-wide membership organisation for all those concerned with adoption, fostering and child care issues.

Contents

◉ Introduction

If you are reading this book or having it read aloud to you, your family is probably planning to adopt a new brother or sister and you want to find out more about adoption and what it will mean for you.

Or, like Ellie, perhaps you already have an adopted brother or sister. Ellie says:

Adoption means belonging to your new family when you can't live with the family you were born into. Franco is my adopted brother now and he is part of our family.

If your family is thinking about adoption you will probably learn some new words. In this book, words that may be new to you have been written in **blue** text. You can find out what they mean at the end of this book. You will see that the words are in alphabetical order.

Ellie has drawn a picture of her family and her mum has put it in this frame.

Franco joined Ellie's family three years ago, when he was two years old. Now he is five years old and he is Ellie's little brother and she is his big sister. They will always be brother and sister, even when they are grown up.

Ellie has quite a large family but Franco is her only brother.

Some families are even bigger and have lots of children!

And some families are very small.

Some families have one parent and some have two parents.

Some families are black and some are white and some are black and white.

All kinds of families may want to adopt a child.

Who is in your family now? Do you want to put them into this frame?

◉ Why are we going to adopt?

Why do families decide to adopt? Families decide to adopt because adoption is one way for parents to have more children and for children who cannot live with their parents, to grow up in a family. Adoption is also a way for children to have more brothers and sisters.

Ellie's mum and dad wanted to adopt because they wanted a bigger family. At first Ellie wasn't at all sure whether she wanted to have a new brother or sister. She was used to having her mum and dad all to herself. She thought: '*Why do they want another child when they've got me?*' Her mum said it was good for families to grow. And Ellie saw that nearly all her friends had brothers and sisters, and they seemed to like each other even when they argued and fought.

Ellie and her dad made a list of all the good things about adoption and a list of all the things Ellie wanted to know more about. This is Ellie's list of all the good things about adoption:

The good things

Having someone special to play with
Having someone to grow up with
Having someone to share secrets with
Having someone who will stick up for me
Having more fun as a family

Here is Ellie's list of the things she wanted to know more about:

What I want to know about adoption

Can we choose a girl or a boy?
Where do adopted children come from?
Where are their mums and dads?
Can they come and take my new brother or sister away again?
Other mums have babies so why don't we?
Will I have to share all my toys and get them broken?
Will mum and dad love me as much if they adopt more children?
Will mum and dad be too busy to take as much notice of me as before?
What if my new brother or sister doesn't like me or I don't like them?

Can you make a list of all the good things about adoption and a list of the things that you want to know more about? Perhaps you could ask a grown-up to help you.

My list of the good things about adoption

_____

_____

_____

_____

_____

_____

_____

Now make a list of all the things you want to know about adoption:

My list of the things about adoption I want to know more about

_____

_____

_____

_____

_____

_____

_____

Is your list like Ellie's list or is it very different? If we look at all of Ellie's questions, we may answer some of yours.

A brother or a sister or both?

When mums have babies, they can't choose whether it's going to be a girl or a boy. If you adopt you might be able to choose, although most families don't mind which they have.

Sometimes Ellie thought a sister would be best and sometimes she thought a brother would be more fun.

Sometimes she wished for an older brother who could take her out, and sometimes she wished for a younger brother she could help to look after.

Sometimes she thought she would like to have a brother and sister all at once.

Ellie says that Franco turned out to be better than all the brothers and sisters she imagined. She enjoys having someone to play with and look after and thinks that Franco is a great little brother.

Can you close your eyes and imagine a brother or a sister?

Do you want to put whom you imagine into this frame?

⦿ Where do adopted children come from?

All children are born to two parents: a mother and a father who are their birth parents.

But sometimes parents cannot look after the children who are born to them and social workers have to find new families for them.

All children need to grow up in a family with a parent or parents who will love them and care for them, help them to be happy and healthy, and keep them safe. When children need new parents, a family just like yours may adopt them.

Ellie's family adopted Franco when he was two years old because his birth parents couldn't manage to have a proper home and keep Franco warm and fed. They were very young and not ready to be parents. Franco was quite a poorly and unhappy toddler when he was adopted, but after he settled down in his new family he showed that he could be a bouncy, jolly little boy when he was happy.

Just sometimes, very little babies need new families if their birth parents can't take care of them.

But most often, children who need new families are even older than Franco when they are adopted; they have probably lived with **foster families** while social workers tried to help their birth parents; but they couldn't help them enough to become good parents.

Ellie says this is what all good parents must do:

Hug their children and play with them
Buy food and clothes and toys
Make home warm and cosy
Cook and clean and go to work to earn money
Take children to school to learn and to the doctor
when they are not well
Teach children right from wrong

What do **you** think good parents should do?

_____

_____

_____

_____

_____

_____

_____

◉ Where are their mums and dads?

Children do not lose their birth parents when they are adopted. But their birth parents will be more like relatives they may or may not see occasionally, or they may write letters and send cards to each other.

How do **you** keep in touch with relatives who live a long way from your house?

A social worker brings Ellie's brother, Franco, a birthday card and letter from his birth mother once a year. Franco can't read yet, so mum reads the letters and cards to him and keeps them for him in a special folder Ellie has made for him.

Franco draws a picture for his birth mother during the summer holidays and mum sends it with a letter all about Franco and with a photo taken on his birthday.

me!

When Franco is older he may want to see his birth mother, and his new family will help him to meet her.

Franco can't keep in touch with his birth father because he went away and no one knows where he is. But Franco has a **life story book** with pictures of his birth family and the story of his life so far. Ellie likes to look at this book with Franco. She has asked her mum to help her to write her own life story and she is sticking in photographs of when she was a baby.

⊙ Can they come and take my new sister or brother away again?

When the judge says your new brother or sister is adopted, they will belong to your family just as you do. They will be your real brother or sister and your parents will be their real parents. And all your grandmas and grandpas and aunts and uncles and cousins will be their grandmas and grandpas and aunts and uncles and cousins too.

No one can take adopted children away from their new families.

Ellie has added Franco to her family tree.

⊙ Other mums have babies so why don't we?

Sometimes mums and dads can't have as many babies as they want to have. They may try to get doctors to help them or they may decide to adopt. Having babies and adopting are both good ways of building families. They are different ways but both ways are good ways.

Some parents feel that they are lucky to have had children born to them and now they want to offer a home and a family to a child who needs them.

Ellie's parents saw Franco's picture in a newspaper that said he needed a new family. They asked the social worker about him and after a lot of preparation they adopted him.

Ellie wondered whether any of her friends' brothers and sisters were adopted.

She told her friends about Franco and one of her best friends, Hannah, said:

'We adopted my older sister before I was even born.'

Ellie liked Hannah's older sister and she was glad that she could talk to Hannah about adoption.

This is a picture Ellie drew of Hannah and her adopted sister.

Do **you** know if any of your friends have an adopted brother or sister?

Will I have to share all my toys and get them broken?

Brothers and sisters don't have to share everything. If you have favourite toys that are precious or you are afraid they might get broken, you can ask your mum or dad to find you a special place to keep them safe. But generally it can be fun to play together with each other's toys. Don't forget that if you share, this will teach your new brother or sister that it is fun to play together, and they might also have toys you want to play with.

All children sometimes fight and argue about who can play with what or who had it first! You will probably squabble with your adopted brother or sister just like other children do, and your parents will get just as cross as all parents do when their children bicker – especially if you make too much noise about it.

Ellie's brother, Franco, didn't really know how to play and share when he first came because he had never had his own toys before. He held on tight to all his belongings because he was afraid someone would take them away again. Ellie let him play with some of her toys (not her best dolls) and Franco learned that it was more fun to play together – but it took quite a long time before he let Ellie touch any of his things.

Do you have any special toys you want to keep out of reach like Ellie's dolls?

Will mum and dad love me as much if they adopt more children?

Of course they will!

Love is unending and you can't measure it. It is like water coming out of a tap that is never turned off or the grains of sand blowing in the desert that no one can count.

When we learn to love somebody new it doesn't mean that we love someone else less. You don't love your mum less because you also love your dad. And you don't love your mum and dad less because you also love your grandma and grandpa.

Parents don't love their children less when a new child is born or when a new child is adopted. And they don't love one child more than another, but all children are different and parents may show their love in different ways.

Ellie liked to have lots of hugs and cuddles with both her parents.

Franco was shy of men because he wasn't used to a dad, and to begin with he didn't like being touched because he had been hurt by other grown-ups.

Mum and dad loved them both, so they cuddled and hugged Ellie and showed Franco how much they cared by listening to him and understanding his feelings.

Will mum and dad be too busy to take as much notice of me as before?

Every new arrival in the family means more work. Your mum and dad might be very busy when you first adopt because it may take time for your new brother or sister to settle down. But don't worry, things will get back to normal.

You can also help your adopted brother or sister to get used to your family by being patient and kind when they make mistakes or when they seem to demand too much attention. They have probably had too little attention in the past and are trying to make up for it.

Don't forget, adoption is a family business and **you** are an important part of it, so expect to be more busy yourself for a while!

Ellie thought she had never had so much to do. She helped her mum with the shopping at the weekend because there was now much more to carry; she watched Franco and kept him occupied while mum got the tea; she helped dad put Franco to bed and they read his bedtime story together. When her friends came to play, Ellie tried to make sure that Franco was neither left out nor messed up their games. Sometimes mum or dad had to come and sort him out.

Ellie made a list of all her new tasks:

Help with Shopping
Look after Franco at teatime
Help dad put Franco to bed and read to him
Let Franco play with me and my friends

How do you think **you** could help when you adopt?

⊙ What if my new brother or sister doesn't like me or I don't like them?

You may not love each other straight away just as you may not like someone to begin with who turns out to be your best friend in the end. It takes time for friendships to grow and love has to grow too.

Think how it must feel to come into a strange family and a strange home and a strange neighbourhood and perhaps also to a strange school. It might make you feel angry and scared at the same time if you can't quite understand what is happening and it might make you behave rather badly. It can be hard to like someone who is behaving badly, especially if you think they are also upsetting your mum and dad.

There may be times when you wish you hadn't adopted a brother or a sister, and it's OK to feel like that. You don't have to pretend that you are happy when you are not. It will make you feel better if you tell your mum and dad about it.

It's true that love can grow but don't expect it to grow too quickly.

Ellie was worried when Franco first came because he was often either sad or angry and he didn't seem to care about her. But, after a few weeks he suddenly said to her: "**I is your 'bother'**". Ellie laughed and picked him up and whirled him round and fell in love with him forever. But she still gets fed up with him when he behaves badly.

Now it is Franco's fifth birthday and Ellie has made him a card.

The journey to adoption

If your family decides to adopt, you go on a kind of journey together. You don't travel to another place, but you learn about adoption and how to welcome a new child into your family.

The people who help families to adopt are called **social workers**. Social workers find new families for children who need them. They talk to everyone in the family about adoption and listen to what everyone has to say. That way they make sure that this is a good family to adopt a child.

If everyone agrees, the social workers write a report for the **Adoption Panel**. This panel is made up of people who know all about adoption. If the adoption panel agree with the report, they will ask the social worker to **approve** the family to adopt.

After a family has been approved, it may take quite a long time before they and the social workers find the right child or children to adopt. Every child is different and every family is different, so it is important to **match** them up together.

Introductions follow once the right child has been matched with the right family. It isn't like being introduced to someone at a party; it is for you and your family and the child you want to adopt to get used to each other and to get ready to live together. This will mean lots of visits and outings and usually takes many weeks.

When a child finally joins a new family, it is called a **placement**. While the family settles down together, the social workers will visit and answer any questions or sort out any problems.

The last bit of the adoption journey is when the whole family goes to **Court** where the **Judge** will make an **Adoption Order**, which means that you now have your very own brother or sister.

For Ellie it was a journey with many stops and waits that seemed to go on forever. She often got impatient and sometimes she got upset because she wanted a brother or a sister **now**. 'But in the end,' she said, 'Franco was worth waiting for'.

Each adoption journey is different and some take longer than others. Ellie and the social workers made a chart of her family's adoption journey. Opposite, you will see what they have drawn.

Perhaps **you** could get a large sheet of paper and ask someone to help you to make a chart of your adoption journey. How far have you and your family gone on your own adoption journey?

Ellie's adoption journey

We meet the Judge and she says that we are Franco's new family. He is now my brother and we have a party

Franco comes to live with us

Franco comes for a sleepover

Franco comes for tea

I meet Franco and we go to the park

Mum and dad meet Franco at his foster mum's house

Mum and dad go to a meeting and we are matched with Franco

The social worker tells us about Franco

Mum and dad are approved

Mum and dad go to adoption classes

Social worker comes to see us. Social worker talks to me on my own

Mum and dad call social worker

Mum and dad talk to me about adoption

start

And finally...

If you have other questions that Ellie did not think of, you should ask your mum or dad or one of the social workers. If you have any worries about adoption, it is really OK to let the grown-ups know. You are an important member of your family and what you think and feel matters.

When you adopt, you are opening your family circle to welcome in a new brother or sister.

On this last page of the book, would you like to draw a circle and write in the names of all the people you can think of in your family? If you want, you can ask someone to help you.

Make sure that you leave a space for your new brother or sister. And now make an opening so that you can help them to get in!

Good luck to you and your family.

⊙ Words that may be new to you

A placement is when a child is placed with a new family and before the adoption is made legal. During this time social workers will visit to sort out any problems and give any help they can. It is a good time to talk about anything that might be bothering you.

Adoption orders rule that the adopted child is now a legal member of their new family. They have the same place in the family as children who are born to the parents.

Adoption panels are made up of a group of people who work in adoption agencies, who have adopted or have been adopted themselves. People on the panel read the reports the social workers have written and meet the families who apply to adopt.

Approval happens when the family is told by the social worker that they can adopt.

Court is a place where rules are made. When a court makes rules they are legal and must not be broken. The people who make the rules in court are called judges. When children are adopted, the whole family usually goes to court for the Adoption Hearing.

Foster homes are ordinary family homes, chosen by social workers, where children live if their birth parents can't take care of them. If they can't go back to their parents, they may be adopted or stay in the foster home for a long time. The people who look after children in foster homes are called foster carers.

Introductions begin after the match has been approved. An introduction can be long or short depending on how long it takes to get to know each other and on where the new child is living – usually in a foster home. A special introduction plan is agreed to suit each child and family.

Judges make the rules about adoption. Judges usually work in special rooms in courts called chambers. Sometimes they wear black gowns and white wigs and sometimes they let the children try on their wig. Judges read all the papers about each adoption and then they sign an important paper called an Adoption Order.

Life story books tell the story of your adopted brother or sister before they came to live with you. They are the record of the important things that have happened to your adopted brother or sister and can include drawings and photographs of people and things that are special to them.

Matching means that the family, the social workers and the adoption panel think carefully about which child to link with which family. The adoption agency has to approve the match before introductions can start.

Social workers are trained to look after people who need help. They help families to deal with problems. Some of them work in adoption agencies and find new families for children who cannot live with their birth parents.